Sales and Use Tax Accounting

Steven M. Bragg

AccountingTools®

ISBN 978-1-64221-286-0

For more information about AccountingTools® products, visit our Web site at www.accountingtools.com.

Table of Contents

About the Author

Steven Bragg, CPA, has been the chief financial officer or controller of four companies, as well as a consulting manager at Ernst & Young. He received a master's degree in finance from Bentley College, an MBA from Babson College, and a Bachelor's degree in Economics from the University of Maine. He has been a two-time president of the Colorado Mountain Club, and is an avid alpine skier, mountain biker, and certified master diver. Mr. Bragg resides in Centennial, Colorado. He has written more than 300 books and courses, including *New Controller Guidebook, GAAP Guidebook*, and *Payroll Management*.

Steven maintains the accountingtools.com web site, which contains continuing professional education courses, the Accounting Best Practices podcast, and thousands of articles on accounting subjects.

Sales and Use Tax Accounting

Introduction

There are more than 11,000 sales tax jurisdictions in the United States, as noted in the following table. Many of these jurisdictions tax the same transactions differently. Given the multitude of sales tax variations, it should be no surprise that the United States is considered one of the most challenging sales tax environments in the world.

Number of Sales Tax Jurisdictions in the United States[1]

State	Total Sales Tax Jurisdictions	State	Total Sales Tax Jurisdictions
Alabama	805	Missouri	1,491
Alaska	109	Nebraska	252
Arizona	131	Nevada	19
Arkansas	400	New Jersey	2
California	401	New Mexico	145
Colorado	305	New York	78
Connecticut	2	North Carolina	106
District of Columbia	1	North Dakota	154
Florida	67	Ohio	96
Georgia	162	Oklahoma	594
Guam	1	Pennsylvania	3
Hawaii	4	Puerto Rico	79
Idaho	12	Rhode Island	1
Illinois	635	South Carolina	46
Indiana	1	South Dakota	258
Iowa	1,028	Tennessee	129
Kansas	594	Texas	1,659
Kentucky	1	Utah	321
Louisiana	388	Vermont	16
Maine	1	Virginia	175
Maryland	1	Washington	385
Massachusetts	1	West Virginia	62
Michigan	1	Wisconsin	76
Minnesota	98	Wyoming	24
Mississippi	3		

---

[1] Source: taxfoundation.org, data provided is as of 2020

Local governments are under increasing financial pressure, and so are more likely to conduct sales and use tax audits. If a government audit team finds irregularities in a firm's sales and use tax remittances, it can charge significant fines and penalties. Further, business owners can be held liable for these fines and penalties, even if the organization has ceased operations. If the audit team suspects that fraud is involved, it can even recommend the filing of criminal charges against the owners or imposing a lien on the assets of the organization. Consequently, the accountant needs to have a system in place for dealing with these taxes, and with a high degree of transactional accuracy.

Businesses tend to place little emphasis on their sales and use tax systems, as this may initially appear to be an obscure part of the accounting function. Further, there is some cost involved in the proper administration of sales and use taxes, which management may not be willing to pay. We will show in this manual that sales and use taxes are actually a high-risk area that can trigger substantial government penalties if a business does not invest a sufficient amount of resources in it.

In the following pages, we will address the nature of sales and use taxes, the administrative requirements for obtaining a sales tax license, the calculation, accounting for, and payment of sales taxes, sales tax audits, sales tax exemptions, and a number of related issues.

Related Podcast Episode: Episode 229 of the Accounting Best Practices Podcast provides an overview of sales and use taxes. The episode is available at: **accounting-tools.com/podcasts** or **iTunes**

What are Sales and Use Taxes?

A *sales tax* is a tax imposed on the sale of tangible personal property and certain services, and is calculated as a percentage of the sales price. The tax is collected by the entity selling the property to a third party, and is remitted to the applicable government entity at regular intervals. The most common arrangement is to have *state-collected taxes*, where all sales taxes are sent to a state's Department of Revenue, which retains the state portion of each tax and then distributes the remainder to the applicable county and city governments and special taxation districts. *Home-rule* or *self-collected* counties, cities, and special taxation districts mandate that those collecting sales taxes remit the taxes directly to them (which greatly increases the volume of required sales tax reporting).

Sales taxes are a key form of revenue for state, county, and local governments. In fact, only five states do *not* currently impose a sales tax. Those states are Alaska, Delaware, Montana, New Hampshire, and Oregon. Of the states that *do* impose a sales tax, there are eight *single rate* states that impose a single statewide tax rate. This leaves 37 *combined rate* states that allow local government entities to add their own sales taxes to the baseline state sales tax rate. Thus, certain locations within a combined rate state could charge a state sales tax, county sales tax, and city sales tax, and perhaps even additional taxes for one or more special districts.

EXAMPLE

The city of Lakewood, Colorado has an overall 7.5% sales tax, which is derived from the following types of sales taxes:

Jurisdiction	Rate
Colorado sales tax	2.9%
Jefferson County sales tax	0.5%
Lakewood sales tax	3.0%
Special district sales tax (two special districts are involved)	1.1%
Total sales tax	7.5%

A person purchases $200 of taxable goods within the city limits of Lakewood and is charged a 7.5% sales tax for a total charge of $215.00. Of the $15.00 of sales tax charged to the person, Colorado receives $5.80 ($200 × 2.9%), Jefferson County receives $1.00 ($200 × 0.5%), the city of Lakewood receives $6.00 ($200 × 3.0%), and the special districts receive $2.20 ($200 × 1.1%).

We have noted that a portion of a sales tax may be allocated to a special district. These districts are intended to collect sales taxes to pay for a specific type of activity. A special district tax may be short-term, lasting only until an underlying expenditure has been paid off. Examples of special districts are:

- Cultural activities district, to support the arts community.
- Stadium district, to pay for the construction of a football, baseball, or other stadium.
- Health services district, to support low-income or no-income health care.
- Local improvement district, to pay for many types of local infrastructure.
- Regional transportation district, to pay for buses, light rail, and so forth.

A business must collect sales taxes if nexus (see the Sales Tax Nexus section) is present. If not, the entity buying the goods or services is instead liable to the government for this tax. However, if the buyer pays the tax, it is now called a *use tax*, rather than a sales tax. The amount to be paid is the tax rate applicable to the buyer's location, and the tax is paid to the government entity with jurisdiction over the buyer's location.

What is Tangible Personal Property?

We just noted that sales taxes are charged on the sale of tangible personal property. Tangible personal property is everything other than real estate that is used in a business or rental property. Examples of tangible personal property are listed in the following exhibit.

Examples of Tangible Personal Property

Art	Furniture	Machinery
Clothing	Household goods	Signs
Computers	Jewelry	Supplies
Equipment	Leasehold improvements	Tools

What are Taxable Services?

We noted earlier that certain services may be subject to sales tax. Years ago, services were generally considered exempt from taxation. However, as state governments have become more mired in financial troubles, they have limited the range of sales tax exemptions in this area in order to collect more tax revenue. Depending on the state, repair and maintenance, equipment installation, data processing, landscaping, building maintenance, and telecommunication services have all lost their exemptions from taxation.

Sales Tax License

The first step in the process of collecting sales taxes on behalf of a state government is to apply for a *sales tax license*, which is a permit to collect sales taxes on behalf of a government. This can generally be done on-line, after which the government mails the business a printed sales tax license for a nominal fee. The license must be renewed at regular intervals, also for a nominal fee. If there is a change in the type of business ownership, such as switching from a sole proprietorship to a partnership, the state usually requires a new license. A sample sales tax license follows. States typically require that the license be posted in a prominent place.

Sample Colorado Sales Tax License

The key part of the sales tax license is the account number noted on the certificate; the business references this number whenever it remits payments or sends correspondence to the government.

If an organization only does business within a single state, then it only needs a sales tax license from that state. However, if (as noted later in the Sales Tax Nexus section), the firm maintains locations, inventory or personnel in other states, it must also obtain sales tax licenses from those state governments. Also, if a business has more than one physical location within a state from which sales are made, a separate sales tax license must be obtained for each one. Further, if a business generates sales at a location other than its regular business location (such as a craft show), a special event license must be obtained. A variation on the special event license is a multiple events license that is good for a longer period of time, such as one or two years.

An organizer of a multi-vendor event may be able to obtain a special event license in lieu of having each individual participating vendor obtain a separate license. The organizer then collects and remits sales tax on behalf of the vendors.

Sales Tax Calculation

The general process flow for a sales tax transaction is for a business to charge the sales tax to its customers, which the business is then responsible for remitting to the applicable government. This usually means that all sales taxes are sent to the Department of Revenue of the state government, which then forwards that portion of the sales tax owed to the county and city governments to those entities.

To calculate sales tax, use the steps outlined below to set up the correct sales tax for a new customer. For an existing customer, it is only necessary to use the final three steps for the sales tax calculation. These steps are needed to ensure that a business does not over-charge or under-charge a customer for taxes. The procedure is:

1. Determine whether the business has nexus for a customer. Nexus is when you have a place of business within the boundaries of a government jurisdiction, or use your own vehicles to transport goods there, or send your employees into that area on business.
2. If there is nexus, set up the appropriate sales tax percentage in the database record of the customer for which you want to record a sale. This may include the compilation of separate sales tax percentages for the applicable state, county, city, and special taxation district. For example, if the state tax is 4%, the county tax is 1% and the city tax is 2%, then the grand total tax charged to the customer will be 7%; the customer does not see this breakdown of individual taxes by government jurisdiction.
3. If a customer is exempt from sales taxes, make sure that it has sent a valid sales tax exemption certificate (see the Sales Tax Exemptions section). Then create a flag in the database record of the customer that no sales tax is to be charged to it. Also, verify that the items being purchased fall within the requirements of the exemption certificate; if not, sales tax must still be charged, even though there is an exemption certificate on file.

4. Create an invoice to document the sale to the customer. The software should automatically pull the applicable tax rates from the database record for the customer and apply it to the total of all items listed on the invoice.
5. If some customer purchases are exempt from sales taxes, flag these items on the invoice and verify that the calculated sales tax does not include them.
6. Record the sales tax liability in the accounting records. If an invoice is sent to the customer for later payment, the entry is a debit to the accounts receivable account and a credit to the liability account for sales taxes payable. If the customer paid in cash at the point of sale, the entry is a debit to the cash account and a credit to the liability account for sales taxes payable.

Note: It is usually mandatory to separately state the grand total sales tax on an invoice. It is not allowable to state that the sales tax is incorporated into the prices being charged.

In order to receive updates on the correct sales tax percentages, file to do business with the various governments in whose jurisdictions the company has nexus. It may be sufficient to file to do business at the level of the applicable state government.

The sales tax rate to be charged to a customer depends on whether the state government requires sales taxes to be calculated where the sale originates or where the goods are delivered; the concept is incorporated into the following example.

EXAMPLE

Ninja Cutlery operates a retail store. When a customer buys products at this location, he is charged the local 6.75% sales tax, and this tax is then remitted to the state, county, and city governments that have jurisdiction over the store location. This is *origin-based* taxation.

Ninja also operates an Internet store. When a customer buys products from the store, Ninja delivers them to the customer's location. Ninja charges the customer the sales tax for the location to which the goods are delivered, and remits the sales tax amount to the state, county, and city governments that have jurisdiction over the delivery location. This is *destination-based* taxation.

If purchased goods are turned over to an independent contractor for delivery to the customer, the store location is considered the point of sale for the purpose of determining sales tax. For example, a buyer acquires carpeting from a carpet supply store that the retailer then turns over to an independent installer for delivery and installation. The sales tax is calculated based on the location of the carpet store.

Sales Tax Accounting

When a customer is billed for sales taxes, the journal entry is a debit to the accounts receivable asset for the entire amount of the invoice, a credit to the sales account for that portion of the invoice attributable to goods or services billed, and a credit to the sales tax liability account for the amount of sales taxes billed.

At the end of the month (or longer, depending on the remittance arrangement with the state), the accountant fills out a sales tax remittance form that states gross sales and sales taxes and sends the government the amount of the sales tax recorded in the sales tax liability account. This remittance may take place before the customer has paid the business for the sales tax. When the customer pays the invoice, the accountant debits the cash account for the amount of the payment and credits the accounts receivable account.

What if the customer does not pay the sales tax portion of the invoice? In that case, the accountant issues a credit memo that reverses the amount of the sales tax liability (and which is also a reduction of the accounts receivable asset account). It is quite likely that the firm will have already remitted this sales tax to the government, so the customer's non-payment becomes a reduction in the firm's next sales tax remittance to the government.

EXAMPLE

International Automation issues an invoice to Lowry Locomotion for $1,000 of goods delivered, on which there is a seven percent sales tax. The entry is:

	Debit	Credit
Accounts receivable	1,070	
Sales		1,000
Sales tax liability		70

Following the end of the month, International remits the sales taxes withheld to the state government. The entry is:

	Debit	Credit
Sales tax liability	70	
Cash		70

Later in the following month, the customer pays the full amount of the invoice. The entry is:

	Debit	Credit
Cash	1,070	
Accounts receivable		1,070

A few states allow a business to retain a small portion of its sales tax collections as a discount. This discount is only made available if the firm remits payments on a timely basis.

Cash or Accrual Basis Accounting

The states allow a business to report gross sales on either the cash basis or the accrual basis of accounting, as long as the method used is consistently applied. Under the cash basis, revenue is recognized when cash is received from customers, and expenses are recognized when payments are made to suppliers and employees. Under the accrual basis, revenue is recognized when earned and expenses when incurred. The accrual basis is a more sophisticated system that requires a knowledgeable accountant, while the cash basis requires a less-skilled bookkeeper. A larger entity always uses the accrual basis, since it is required by the IRS when a firm's gross receipts exceed $5 million per year. In addition, auditors will refuse to render an audit opinion on an organization's financial statements if the cash basis has been used to construct the financials.

Sales Taxes Liability Account

Sales taxes payable is a liability account in which is stored the aggregate amount of sales taxes that a business has collected from customers on behalf of a governing tax authority and has not yet remitted to the government. The business is the custodian of these funds, and is liable for remitting them to the government on a timely basis. It is possible that the sales taxes payable account can be subdivided into a number of accounts, with each one containing the sales taxes applicable to only a particular government entity. For example, one account might be used to store sales taxes for a state government, while another account may be used for the county government, and yet another account for the local city government. If a company is required to collect sales taxes on behalf of many government jurisdictions, this can mean that a company could potentially store sales taxes payable information in a large number of accounts.

Sales Tax Presentation

The sales tax liability account is considered a current liability, since the obligation must be settled within one year. Consequently, it appears in the current liabilities section of the balance sheet, usually shortly after the accounts payable line item. If the sales tax liability balance is a small one, the line item may be lumped into an "other liabilities" line item. A sample presentation of the current liabilities portion of a balance sheet appears in the following exhibit.

Sample Presentation of Sales Tax Liability

LIABILITIES AND EQUITY	20X2	20X1
Current liabilities		
Trade and other payables	$217,000	$198,000
Short-term borrowings	133,000	202,000
Current portion of long-term borrowings	5,000	5,000
Sales taxes payable	26,000	23,000
Accrued expenses	9,000	13,000
Total current liabilities	$390,000	$441,000

Account Reconciliation

A large amount of transactional activity may run through the sales tax liability account, since the sales tax on each customer invoice appears in the account as a separate line item. There will also be periodic offsetting debits to this account whenever sales taxes are remitted to the state government. Given the volume of activity, there is a good chance that an error will creep into the account and be undetected unless the accountant engages in a periodic reconciliation of the account. An account reconciliation involves the following activities:

- Verifying that all sales taxes were charged to the correct account.
- Verifying that all payments were posted to the correct account.
- Determining whether any remittance payments were missed.

Sales Tax Remittances

As part of the application process, an organization will be asked to estimate the amount of taxable sales that it expects to generate. Based on this information, the government will assign a filing frequency of monthly or quarterly. In rare cases where sales tax remittances are minimal, the filing frequency may be reduced to just once a year. In cases where the firm only operates on a seasonal basis, the government may allow it to only file sales tax returns for those months in which the firm is in operation. If the amount of remittances later increases, then the government can increase the required remittance frequency.

It is quite possible that a company may remit sales taxes to the state government when it has not yet been paid by its customers. This is most likely to be the case when the company's credit terms are 30 days or longer and the Department of Revenue requires that the company remit sales taxes to it on a monthly basis. In this situation, when a customer does not pay on time, the company must use its own funds to pay the Department of Revenue, and then collects the sales tax from the customer at a later date. This can cause a cash flow imbalance for the company.

If the company elects to file paper-based returns, the Department of Revenue (depending on the state) sends forms that are preprinted with the company's name, address, account number, and the taxing districts for which sales tax collections are normally made, as well as the due date. The accountant fills out the form and mails it in early enough to ensure that the Department receives the form prior to the due date. A form submission is required even if the amount of sales tax to be remitted is zero. A variation is to file a return and submit a payment electronically, which can be more convenient. Many states require payment by electronic funds transfer when an organization's annual sales tax remittances exceed a certain threshold level, such as $100,000.

> **Note:** When paying the Department of Revenue by check, be sure to write on the check the account number and period for which payment is being submitted. Doing so reduces the risk that a payment will be incorrectly applied to the company's account or to the account of some other business.

Always make a photocopy of every sales tax return and use tax return sent to the government, along with a copy of the check payment. If an electronic filing was made, then print a copy of the payment confirmation. These documents are needed for those situations in which the government takes issue with the company regarding a tax payment, and the firm needs to produce evidence of payment. This situation can arise when the government incorrectly posts a payment to the account of some other business.

Over-Collected Sales Tax

A business may collect an excessively large sales tax amount from a customer. For example, perhaps the wrong sales tax rate was manually applied to an invoice. Or, perhaps sales tax was applied to an invoice line item that was actually exempt from tax. When this situation is discovered, there are two ways to proceed, which are:

- If the excess amount of the sales can be properly documented and the customer can be contacted, then refund the excess amount back to the customer. For example, if the excess tax is $100, the accountant prepares a payment that debits the sales taxes payable account for $100 and credits the cash account for $100.
- If the excess amount cannot be properly documented and it is impossible to find the customer in order to issue a refund, then the excess amount must be forwarded to the Department of Revenue. Under no circumstances does the company retain the excess amount. If it later becomes possible to refund the customer, the accountant files an amended return or claim for refund form (for which a sample follows from the State of Colorado) that requests a refund of the overpayment from the Department of Revenue back to the company. An alternative treatment is to deduct the amount of the overpayment from the next periodic sales tax return. Archive a copy of the amended return along with all supporting documents, in case a later sales tax audit questions the refund.

> **Note:** From a customer relations standpoint, it is generally better to refund a sales tax over-collection to a customer right away, rather than waiting for a refund from the Department of Revenue, which may not be received for several months.

Sample Claim for Refund Form

Claim for Refund

This claim for is for monies remitted directly to the Department of Revenue.
(Do not use for income tax refund)

- For sales and use tax refunds requests please see FYI Sales 90 for instructions.
- For withholding refunds please see FYI Withholding 5 for instructions.
- Claims submitted without proper documentation will be denied.
- The vendor's fee, which was retained when the tax was remitted to the Department, will be deducted from all sales tax refund claims.
- If possible, instead of submitting a claim for refund to the Department, deduct the overpaid taxes on your next tax return or obtain the refund from the seller who collected the tax.
- Submit claim for each type of tax (e.g. state sales, RTD/CD/FD/RTA, city sales, county sales, etc.)
- Periods can be combined if consecutive for each type of tax.
- Submit a copy of this form and keep a copy for your records.
- Interest: If this refund qualifies for interest please provide the interest in the claim and an explanation of how the refund qualifies for interest. See FYI Sales 90 for more information.

Refund to be made payable to, and mailed to:
(If this is different from the name and address on the Department records for the account number(s) used, provide explanation and notarized power of attorney specific to this refund claim for the action.)

Taxpayer Last Name	First Name	Middle Initial
Taxpayer DBA (if applicable)		

Mailing Address	City	State	Zip

SSN	FEIN (required)

Colorado Department of Revenue Account Number	Type of Tax	Period (MM/YY - MM/YY)

Original Amount Paid	Correct Amount	Refund Requested

Reason (Explanation of the reason for the refund request must be entered here.) All supporting documentation must be attached.

I declare under penalty of perjury in the second degree that this claim including all attachments is to the best of my knowledge true and correct.

I further understand that the claim and documentation may be subject to the same verification process used by the Department of Revenue in auditing other taxes for three years from the date of payment of the claim. [13-80-101 (1)(m) C.R.S.]

Taxpayer Signature (this line must be signed by an officer, partner, or owner of the firm claiming the refund)

Title	Phone Number	Date (MM/DD/YY)

Signature of Preparer (if other than taxpayer)

Name of Firm	Phone Number	Date (MM/DD/YY)

Under-Collected Sales Tax

Another scenario is that the company has under-collected sales tax from a customer, perhaps because the rate used was too low or the rate was not applied to some line items on an invoice. No matter what the reason, the company is still responsible for remitting the full amount to the Department of Revenue. This means that the company will have to pay the amount of the under-collected sales tax. The accountant may be able to pursue collection of this amount from the customer, or the company will have to absorb the cost. In many cases, the management team may decide that they do not want to interfere with a good customer relationship, and so elects to absorb the cost of the under-collected tax.

In some cases, the accountant will not become aware of an under-collection problem until after a sales tax return has been filed. If so, prepare an amended return (which replaces the original return) and include the amount that was missing from the original payment.

A prime reason for an under-collected sales tax is that the government increased the rate (rarely the reverse) without providing notice to the affected businesses. To keep this issue from causing problems, include on the accounting department's calendar of activities a requirement to check the Department of Revenue's official listing of sales tax rates at least once a year, if not more frequently.

Late Filing Penalties and Interest

If the entity does not file its sales tax returns in a timely manner, the state government can assess penalties and interest that will vary in size, depending on the amount by which each tax return is late. When it is found that a tax return has not been filed, the related interest charge for the unpaid amount of the remittance may continue to accrue for several days, because it takes time for a check payment to clear the bank. To reduce the amount of this charge, consider using an ACH payment or wire transfer, which shortens the interval before the government receives payment.

Note: Even when there are no taxable sales to report in a reporting period, always file a tax return. Otherwise, the Department of Revenue will assume that the business has missed a tax payment.

If the business had a valid reason for not submitting a sales tax return in a timely manner, it may be possible to have the late filing penalty waived by submitting a written request to the Department of Revenue. Each state has a different procedure for doing so. The following sample request form is used by the North Carolina Department of Revenue. In the form, the government implies that the only reasonable excuses that warrant a waiver are the death or serious illness of the taxpayer or tax preparer or the occurrence of a natural disaster or accident that destroyed the relevant tax records.

Sample Request to Waive Penalties

NCDOR | NC-5500
Web-Fill
12-24
Request to Waive Penalties

PRINT   CLEAR

Part 1. Taxpayer Information

| Individual's First Name | M.I. | Individual's Last Name | Individual's Social Security Number |

| Spouse's First Name *(If joint return filed)* | M.I. | Spouse's Last Name *(If joint return filed)* | Spouse's Social Security Number *(if joint return filed)* |

| Individual's Phone Number | Individual's Email Address |

| Entity's Legal Name | Entity's Federal Employer ID Number |

| Entity's Trade Name | Account Number/NCDOR ID |

| Contact Person's Name | Contact Person's Phone Number |

| Contact Person's Email Address |

| Street Address |

| City | State | Zip Code |

Part 2. Waiver Information *Enter the requested information below for each notice that you are requesting penalty relief.*

Tax Type	Notice Number	Period Beginning	Period Ending	Amount of Penalty	Reason for Request

Part 3. Explanation of Reason *Check the box for each reason listed above and enter the requested information. Attach additional pages if necessary.*

☐ **Good Compliance.** *(By checking this box, you certify that the above-named taxpayer meets all the conditions necessary to qualify for a good compliance record. See the Department's Penalty Policy.)*

☐ **Death.** *(The decedent must be the taxpayer, the taxpayer's immediate family member, or the taxpayer's tax preparer. In addition, the death must have occurred within 3 months before the due date of the tax for which the penalty was charged.)*

Name of deceased: _____

Date of death: _____ Relationship to taxpayer: _____

Explain how the death prevented compliance with tax law. Include any documentation that you believe supports your request for penalty relief.

_____

_____

Response to Notice of Non-Filing

It is possible that the accounting staff will forget to submit a sales tax filing from time to time. If so, the Department of Revenue will issue a non-payment notice to the firm.

Upon receipt of this notice, the accountant should immediately determine whether a payment was actually made, and if the check cleared the bank. If so, print copies of both sides of the check and forward it to the Department of Revenue as proof that the issue is on their side, not the company's. Or, if the payment was made electronically, send the electronic confirmation sheet instead. In this case, the Department of Revenue most likely credited the payment to the account of some other business. If so, the company is not at fault for the "late" payment, and the accountant should file for the reversal of any assessed penalties and interest.

> **Note:** When sending documents to the Department of Revenue, be sure to include in the mailing a complete set of documents, including the initial notice, the issue under dispute, and any supporting evidentiary matter. Also, retain a copy of this mailing, in case someone from the Department calls to discuss the issue. The copy should be retained for several years, in case the issue is ever brought up again.

Another possibility is that the accountant filled out and submitted the sales tax return for the wrong month. This happens when a business is issued a preprinted set of documents, each for a different month of the year. For example, the accountant might mistakenly submit the sales tax return for October when he meant to submit the return for September. When this happens, the Department of Revenue may credit the payment to the month stated on the return, which is the wrong month. If so, call the Department, notify them of the filing mistake, and have them shift the payment amount into the correct reporting period. Also, ask them what to do when it is time to file a return for the reporting period for which the form was just mistakenly used.

It is also possible that the submission was sent to the Department of Revenue too late to meet the Department's filing deadline. If so, pay the assessed penalties and interest without complaint (since the company was at fault) and proceed to an examination of the reason for the late payment. It is essential to make whatever procedural change is necessary to ensure that a late payment is not made again.

If it appears that no payment was sent, then clearly the first step is to prepare the sales tax return and use a rush delivery to send it to the Department of Revenue. Once this has been done, the accountant will need to determine the reason for the non-payment. Some possibilities are:

- The task was left off the department calendar
- The person responsible for the task left the company or switched jobs
- The payment was included in a check run that was later than the state's cutoff date

It is critical to install a procedural change to eliminate the underlying problem. Making no change and simply assuming that the problem will not recur is not sufficient – the chances will then be excellent that the accounting staff will fail to file the return again at some future date.

> **Note:** When calling the Department of Revenue about non-filing issues, write down the name of the person contacted, the date, and what was discussed. This information can be useful in subsequent conversations with the Department, to build a history of how each issue is being dealt with.

Sales Tax Nexus

Nexus is the physical presence of a business in a state. Whenever nexus can be established, the company must charge customers for taxes related to that taxing authority and remit the collected taxes to the taxing entity. Given the multitude of taxing entities in the United States, it makes sense to minimize nexus, thereby reducing the number of tax remittance and reporting obligations of the business. As a general rule, an out-of-state business will have nexus in a state if it has regular and systematic contacts within the state, primarily through its employees, agents, or property. More specifically, nexus is considered to have been established if any one of the following conditions can be proven:

- A company maintains a facility of any type within the borders of the state, such as a warehouse or office.
- A company pays the wages of an employee located within the borders of the state.
- Company employees travel to the state to solicit business there, such as flying in a salesperson to meet with a prospective customer.
- A parent company has a subsidiary located within the state.
- A company has Internet marketing affiliates within the state that provide links on their websites back to the company's website.

Some taxing authorities have expanded the definition of nexus in order to generate more tax revenue. Their view includes the preceding items, plus the following ones:

- A company uses its own vehicles to transport goods inside the borders of the taxing authority.
- A company sells data from a server that is physically located within the borders of the taxing authority (even if the server is owned by a third party).

Another possibility is economic nexus, which is covered in the next section.

Given these differences in what constitutes nexus, it is best to contact the local state government for the applicable rules regarding it.

> **Note:** It is possible to register with a state in order to collect sales taxes, even if the business does not have nexus within the state.

<u>Tax Remittances Required Under Nexus</u>

If nexus exists, a company must take the following steps:

- File with the local state government to do business within the state, which requires a small annual filing fee
- Apply for a state sales tax license
- Withhold sales taxes on all sales made within the region
- Remit the sales taxes to the applicable government entity
- Pay personal property taxes on any assets located within the region

<u>Nexus Avoidance</u>

The main effect of nexus is that it requires a significant amount of time by the accounting staff to keep track of tax rates, adjust customer billings, and remit taxes. These activities can add to the administrative headcount, so there is general resistance to having nexus applied to a business by yet another taxing authority. Nexus avoidance can even be an active planning process that may include the avoidance of company-owned delivery vehicles and avoiding the use of facilities in certain states that are known for being particularly aggressive about collecting sales taxes.

The South Dakota vs. Wayfair Case (Economic Nexus)

The Supreme Court handed down a major decision involving sales taxes in 2018, where it stated in the *South Dakota vs. Wayfair* case that South Dakota could apply its sales tax to Internet retailers, even when they have no property or employees in the state. The Court was ruling specifically on the South Dakota sales tax law, pointing out that this specific law was no burden to interstate commerce, given that it did not impose an obligation to remit sales taxes retroactively and imposed a simplified tax rate structure.

The Wayfair case means that the concept of *economic nexus* is now a major issue for anyone selling to customers located in another state. Economic nexus is created when a business generates a certain amount of sales in a particular state. Some state governments measure this figure based on the overall dollar amount of transactions generated, while others combine the concept with the total number of individual sales transactions completed. It is an open question as to how low a state can go in setting economic nexus thresholds, since very low thresholds make it more difficult for small businesses to administer.

The ramifications of economic nexus are clearly more administrative work for mid- to large-sized companies that sell across state lines (such as any Internet business). This is not especially difficult when a state provides sellers with a consolidated application and administration system, but this is not always the case – some states have quite a disorganized approach to economic nexus, requiring sellers to make separate filings with individual cities and counties. Calculating sales tax is a particular concern in the latter case, where a seller may have to deal with hundreds or even thousands of different sales tax rates. Individual states are still deciding how to handle the economic nexus concept. The following table shows the current status of the situation in each state.

Economic Nexus Rules by State[2]

State	Current Status	Threshold Level(s)	Includable Sales
Alabama	In effect	$250,000	Retail sales
Alaska	Some municipalities	$100,000 **or** 200 transactions	Gross sales
Arizona	In effect	$100,000	Gross sales
Arkansas	In effect	$100,000 **or** 200 transactions	Taxable sales
California	In effect	$500,000	Gross sales
Colorado	In effect	$100,000	Retail sales
Connecticut	In effect	$100,000 **and** 200 transactions	Gross sales
District of Columbia	In effect	$100,000 **or** 200 transactions	Retail sales
Florida	In effect	$100,000	Taxable sales
Georgia	In effect	$100,000 **or** 200 transactions	Retail sales
Hawaii	In effect	$100,000 **or** 200 transactions	Gross sales
Idaho	In effect	$100,000	Gross sales
Illinois	In effect	$100,000 **or** 200 transactions	Retail sales
Indiana	In effect	$100,000	Gross sales
Iowa	In effect	$100,000	Gross sales
Kansas	In effect	$100,000	Gross sales
Kentucky	In effect	$100,000 **or** 200 transactions	Retail sales
Louisiana	In effect	$100,000	Retail sales
Maine	In effect	$100,000 **or** 200 transactions	Gross sales
Maryland	In effect	$100,000 **or** 200 transactions	Gross sales
Massachusetts	In effect	$100,000	Gross sales
Michigan	In effect	$100,000 **or** 200 transactions	Gross sales
Minnesota	In effect	$100,000 **or** 200 transactions	Retail sales
Mississippi	In effect	$250,000+	Gross sales
Missouri	In effect	$100,000	Taxable sales
Nebraska	In effect	$100,000 **or** 200 transactions	Retail sales
Nevada	In effect	$100,000 **or** 200 transactions	Retail sales
New Jersey	In effect	$100,000 **or** 200 transactions	Gross sales
New Mexico	In effect	$100,000	Taxable sales
New York	In effect	$500,000 **and** 100 transactions	Gross sales
North Carolina	In effect	$100,000	Gross sales
North Dakota	In effect	$100,000	Taxable sales

---

[2] Information summarized from https://www.salestaxinstitute.com/resources/economic-nexus-state-guide

State	Current Status	Threshold Level(s)	Includable Sales
Ohio	In effect	$100,000 **or** 200 transactions	Retail sales
Oklahoma	In effect	$100,000	Taxable sales
Pennsylvania	In effect	$100,000	Gross sales
Rhode Island	In effect	$100,000 **or** 200 transactions	Gross sales
South Carolina	In effect	$100,000	Gross sales
South Dakota	In effect	$100,000	Gross sales
Tennessee	In effect	$100,000	Retail sales
Texas	In effect	$500,000	Gross sales
Utah	In effect	$100,000 **or** 200 transactions	Gross sales
Vermont	In effect	$100,000 **or** 200 transactions	Gross sales
Virginia	In effect	$100,000 **or** 200 transactions	Retail sales
Washington	In effect	$100,000	Gross sales
West Virginia	In effect	$100,000 **or** 200 transactions	Gross sales
Wisconsin	In effect	$100,000	Gross sales
Wyoming	In effect	$100,000 **or** 200 transactions	Gross sales

The preceding table does not include states that do not charge a sales tax.

The adoption of a threshold level of 200 sales transactions by state governments will likely be the driving factor in determining whether to withhold sales taxes on sales to customers located in those states. This means that the seller will need to start compiling the total number of sales transactions by state, and reviewing it on a monthly basis. The exact rules will vary by state, but assume that sales tax withholdings will need to begin as soon as the 200th transaction has been completed within a calendar year.

EXAMPLE

ABC Retail has just sold its 200th transaction of the year to customers located in Ohio. It is August 13. As of the 201st transaction, which happens to occur on August 16, ABC needs to start withholding sales tax on any additional sales to customers in Ohio, and remitting the proceeds to the state. Now that the 200-transaction threshold has been reached, ABC will need to withhold sales taxes on *all* sales into Ohio on a go-forward basis.

In other cases, the total amount of taxable sales into a state will be the driving issue, rather than the number of transactions. When this is the case, the company will need to compile the total taxable sales volume by state, to see if the threshold level has been reached. When this happens, individual state rules will determine the exact date when sales tax withholding must commence.

A further concern regarding economic nexus is that some states require sales taxes to be paid based on local sales tax rates where individual customers are located, rather than allowing out-of-state sellers to pay a single state-wide rate. This greatly amplifies the sales tax reporting burden, especially for smaller sellers who have barely exceeded the $100,000 or 200-transaction sales thresholds needed to trigger sales tax withholding in most states.

> **Tip:** If a state has a voluntary disclosure program, a seller should use it, since doing so reduces the state's look-back period and minimizes penalties for sales taxes not collected in prior periods.

Sales Tax Exemptions

The application of sales tax to *all* sale transactions is by no means a comprehensive requirement. Instead, each government jurisdiction has its own rules for which types of sales may be excluded from the calculation of sales tax, such as for the sale of food. This can make it difficult for a business to keep track of sales tax inclusions and exclusions on an ongoing basis. The number of exemptions can be quite massive, as indicated by the following list extracted from the sales and use tax exemptions list for the state of Colorado (please note that this is not even the complete list, which is 20 pages long). It can be instructive to peruse the topics in this list of exemptions in order to gain a feel for the types of transactions that may (or may not) be subject to sales or use tax:

- A subscription fee for access to comparative performance ratings and emerging stocks is a service, and so is not subject to sales tax.
- Alteration services are not taxable if separable from the sale of clothing.
- Assets acquired by a secured lender through foreclosure are not subject to sales tax, though a subsequent sale of the assets would be subject to sales tax.
- Authentication services via a digital certificate are not subject to sales tax.
- Call center services are non-taxable services.
- Components purchased for manufactured products are exempt, because the products are then intended to be sold.
- Computer software that is used by a consumer via an application service provider is not taxable computer software, because the software is not considered to be delivered to the consumer in a tangible medium.
- Computer software updates that are delivered electronically are not subject to sales tax because they are not tangible personal property.
- Education and training is a non-taxable service.
- Electric service provider's internal use of electricity is not taxable, since it is not being sold.
- Employment recruitment services are non-taxable services.
- Firewood and propane sales for residential use are exempt from sales tax.
- Food that has a "nutritional facts" label is exempt from sales tax.
- Fuel sales for industrial purposes are exempt from sales tax.
- Infusion pumps that administer medications are exempt from sales tax if prescribed by a licensed provider.
- Live web seminars are not subject to sales tax because the seminar is a service. A pre-recorded web seminar and self-study material online are subject to tax.

- Meal charges by a residential retirement community to its residents are exempt from sales tax.
- Medical record retrieval and copying is a service, so it is not subject to sales tax.
- Mobile homes are not subject to sales tax if they are so permanently attached to real property at the time of sale that they are treated as real property.
- Orthotics, braces and splints are exempt from sales tax if furnished to the patient by a licensed provider as part of the provider's professional service.
- Prepaid gasoline charges relating to the lease of a motor vehicle are not taxable as long as the charges are separately stated and optional.
- Reimbursable expenses to be billed to a client are not subject to sales tax, unless the reimbursement is considered a resale of taxable goods.
- Sales made to a Native American tribal member are exempt from sales tax if the sale occurs on the tribal member's tribal land. Sales to non-tribal members on tribal land are not exempt.
- Transportation services are exempt from sales tax.
- Video production is a non-taxable sale of services.
- Virtual lessons are a service, and so are not subject to taxation.
- Water sold through a pipeline is not subject to sales tax, though bulk water sales sold in tanks are subject to sales tax.
- Web collaboration services provided to consumers within the state by means of servers located outside the state are not subject to sales tax, because it is an interstate service.
- Website hosting by an out-of-state company when the servers are also located out-of-state is not taxable.

Note: An item may be listed by a state government as exempt from sales tax, and yet can still be subject to city, county or special district sales tax if these jurisdictions choose not to grant a similar exemption.

In cases where there is a legitimate sales tax exemption, be sure to state the exempt item separately from the rest of the contents of a billing, to clarify the items to which sales tax is and is not being applied. For example, a furniture company sells disassembled furniture to its customers and also offers to assemble the furniture on-site for an additional labor charge. The billing should separate the cost of the furniture from the assembly labor, so that customers will only be charged sales tax for the disassembled furniture.

Private Letter Rulings

The list of sales tax exemptions that a state's Department of Revenue publishes may not contain a reference to an organization's exact situation, making it more difficult to determine which transactions are taxable. In this situation, the firm can request a private letter ruling on its specific situation. A *private letter ruling* is a specific determination of the tax consequences of a proposed or completed transaction. A private letter ruling is generally binding on the issuing jurisdiction, and so provides taxpayers with greater certainty regarding how to proceed. However, a private letter ruling can only be relied upon by the party to whom the ruling was issued, not other taxpayers. To request a private letter ruling, the following information should be assembled and forwarded to the applicable Department of Revenue:

- A statement that a ruling is being requested
- A complete statement of all relevant facts
- A discussion of the business reasons for the transaction
- Copies of all documents relevant to the ruling
- Identification of the taxpayer, including the entity's name, address and federal employment identification number

Note: The Department of Revenue may charge a fee to create a private letter ruling, which is usually based on its estimate of the number of hours that will be required to review a transaction and formulate a ruling. A more complex ruling may require a non-refundable advance payment of several thousand dollars.

Always keep all private letter rulings on file, since they can be used as a valid defense if related sales tax transactions are later questioned by a sales tax auditor.

Note: State governments typically post private letter rulings on their websites (with the identifying names blanked out), so it can make sense to peruse these rulings to see if an applicable situation has already received a ruling by the government.

Sales Tax Exemption Certificates

A business may not be required to pay sales taxes under either of two scenarios, which are as follows:

- *Usage basis.* The state government has declared that, as long as a product is used in a certain way, no sales tax will be charged. For example, fuel purchased for industrial use may be considered tax-exempt, but if the fuel is then taken by an employee for personal use, the designated usage exemption is being avoided, and use tax should be paid. The most common usage basis for a sales tax exemption is when the buyer of goods intends to include them in the production of its own products, which will then be sold to another party. In this case, only the final customer is required to pay sales tax.
- *Entity exemption.* The state government has declared that certain types of organizations do not have to pay sales taxes. The most common of these entities are religious, government, and non-profit organizations. The government may issue a separate type of exemption certificate to these entities, such as a non-profit certificate of exemption. There are also industry-specific exemptions, such as the agricultural exemption certificate issued by Kansas that appears in the following exhibit, where a farmer is exempt from purchases used in the conduct of his business.

Sample Agricultural Exemption Certificate

KANSAS DEPARTMENT OF REVENUE
466318
AGRICULTURAL EXEMPTION CERTIFICATE

Seller Name: _____

Seller Address: _____
        Street   City   State   Zip Code

Purchaser Name: _____

Purchaser Address: _____
        Street   City   State   Zip Code

Provide a description of tangible property or services purchased: _____

_____

PART A (required) - QUALIFYING EXEMPTION

Check all that apply.

☐ Property purchased is an ingredient or component part. Complete Part D. [see K.S.A. 79-3606(m)]

☐ Property purchased is consumed in production. Complete Part D. [see K.S.A. 79-3606(n)]

☐ Property purchased is propane for agricultural use. Complete Part D. [see K.S.A. 79-3606(w)]

☐ Property purchased is farm machinery and equipment or aquaculture machinery and equipment, repair and replacement parts therefor or services performed in repair and maintenance of such machinery and equipment, which will be used exclusively in farming, ranching, or aquaculture production. If property is a work-site utility vehicle. Complete Part C. [see K.S.A. 79-3606(t)]

☐ Property purchased is seed, tree seedling, fertilizer, insecticide, herbicide, germicide, pesticide, fungicide, or services, purchased and used for the purpose of producing plants in order to prevent soil erosion on land devoted to agricultural use. Complete Part D. [see K.S.A. 79-3606(mm)]

☐ Property purchased is tangible personal property or services necessary to construct, reconstruct, repair, or replace any fence that is used to enclose land devoted to agricultural use. Complete Part B. [see K.S.A. 79-3606d(b)]

PART B - FENCING

Location of agriculture land: _____
                    City   State   Zip Code   County

Name of agricultural landowner or operator: _____

☐ By checking this box, I certify that I have read the instructions included on the back of this form and the tangible personal property or services purchased will be used to enclose land which is devoted to agricultural use only and I acknowledge that any tangible personal property or service purchased which is not used exclusively to enclose land devoted for agricultural use is subject to Kansas sales tax. Complete Part D.

PART C - WORK-SITE UTILITY VEHICLE

Confirm that the purchased vehicle has all the following specifications.

☐ Vehicle is **NOT** less than forty-eight (48) inches in width

☐ Vehicle's unladen weight, including fuel, is more than eight hundred (800) pounds

☐ Vehicle is equipped with four or more non-highway tires

☐ Vehicle is equipped with bench or bucket type seating

☐ Vehicle is equipped with bed or cargo box for hauling materials

All five boxes must be checked for the vehicle to qualify for the agricultural exemption.

Select all activities the vehicle will be used for:

☐ Farming   ☐ Ranching   ☐ Agriculture

Describe how the vehicle will be used in each activity selected above: _____

☐ By checking this box, I certify that I have read the instructions included on the back of this form and the vehicle purchased will be used **exclusively** in farming, ranching, or aquaculture production and that using the vehicle in any other activity, such as hunting or other recreational purposes, subjects the vehicle to Kansas sales tax. Complete Part D.

PART D (required) – CERTIFICATION FOR ALL PURCHASERS INCLUDING CONTRACTORS

I declare under penalty of perjury under the law of the State of Kansas that the foregoing is true and correct and that I have read the guidance included on the back of this form. I further understand that in the event the property so purchased is not used in accordance with the exemption checked above, I may be liable for any Kansas sales tax owed and any applicable penalties and interest.

_____   _____   _____
Signature   Print Name   Date

☐ Check this box and sign above as a purchaser, if you are a contractor purchasing materials (tangible personal property) for fencing used to enclose land devoted to agricultural purposes.

ST-28F (Rev. 8-22)

The manner in which an exemption is administratively handled will vary by state. For example, one state might issue certificates of exemption that prevent applicable sales taxes from being charged at the point of sale. Or, another state might require that sales tax be paid at the point of sale, after which organizations may apply to the Department of Revenue for an annual refund. The latter approach carries a higher administrative burden for all parties, but gives the government use of the remitted funds for up to a year.

A business must still pay either sales or use tax on tangible assets that it consumes. For example, a firm might consume the following and pay a tax on them:

- Office supplies
- Office furniture and fixtures
- Office maintenance consumables
- Store shelving
- Store signage

A seller should only skip a sales tax billing to a customer when the customer produces a sales tax exemption form (sometimes called a resale certificate) that has been issued by the local state government. A sample form issued by the state of Nebraska follows. By signing an exemption form, a business is committing to only use purchased goods in the manner claimed on the certificate; if the business uses the goods in some other way, it acknowledges responsibility for then submitting the applicable use tax to the government.

The seller should keep this form on file, in case sales tax auditors question the missing tax. A business may have a large number of these forms on file from its customers; to keep them properly organized, consider storing them in alphabetical order in a three-ring binder. Better yet, scan the forms into a digital format and store them off-site, to prevent their loss if the company's main facility is destroyed. If these forms are not on file, the auditors could hold the seller liable for all tax-free sales.

> **Note:** Examine each exemption certificate when received to ensure that all fields have been completed and the document has been signed. If any information is missing or incomplete, a sales tax auditor could invalidate the certificate. If a customer's certificate is declared invalid, the seller is then responsible for the sales taxes that should have been collected from the customer.

Exemption certificates are only valid for a certain period of time, after which they must be replaced with a new certificate. Check with the applicable state government to determine the termination date for its certificates, and contact customers to obtain new certificates before the termination date is reached.

Tax-free sales should *only* be allowed after a sales tax exemption certificate is on file. If a sales tax auditor finds that an exemption certificate is dated *after* tax-free sales were made to a customer, the auditor can hold the seller liable for the sales tax on those sales.

Sample Resale Certificate

Nebraska Resale or Exempt Sale Certificate for Sales Tax Exemption — FORM 13

A variation on the sales tax exemption certificate is an exemption on the purchase of machinery and machine tools that will be used within the state in a manufacturing process. Though this exemption may be allowed at the state level, local governments such as cities and counties may not grant the exemption, resulting in the payment of a reduced sales tax that does not include the state-level sales tax. To claim the exemption, the accountant fills out a form (such as the one shown in the next exhibit for the state of Colorado) and sends one copy to the seller and one to the applicable state's

Department of Revenue. Upon receipt of the completed form, the seller no longer has any liability to collect sales tax on the sale. Instead, the buyer is now liable for any subsequent sales or use tax liability associated with the purchase.

Sample Form for Machinery-Related Sales Tax Exemption

Sales Tax Exemption On Purchases Of Machinery And Machine Tools				
Seller			Colorado Sales Tax Account Number	
Address	City		State	Zip
Purchaser			Colorado Sales Tax Account Number	
Address	City		State	Zip
Date of Purchase (MM/DD/YY)	Amount of Purchase	Is Equipment ☐ Leased ☐ Purchased		
Description of Item(s) Including Machine Parts				
How Used in Manufacturing				
End Product	How Sold ☐ Wholesale ☐ Retail ☐ New ☐ Used			
This Section is for Businesses Located in Enterprise Zones (See Instructions on Reverse Side)				
Amount of Purchase for Machinery, Machine Tools and Parts				
Materials used in the construction of machinery and machine tools (after 06/07/89)				
I hereby certify that _____ is (Name of Purchasing Firm or Person) entitled to the exemption on purchases of machinery or machine tools.				
Name of Person Authorizing Purchase (please print)				
By (Authorized Signature of Purchasing Firm)		Title		

A final note regarding the use of sales tax exemption forms is that the seller is expected to use common sense when applying it. When a customer is clearly purchasing goods that will not be covered by the terms of its exemption certificate, the seller is still obligated to charge sales tax. For example, when a farmer has an agricultural exemption certificate for the purchase of fertilizer and pesticides, but also buys a lawn chair with the same purchase order, the seller should realize that the lawn chair does not fall under the exemption, and so should be taxed.

Multiple Points of Use Certificate

Sales taxes present a particular problem for those companies that sell and purchase software that is to be concurrently used in multiple tax jurisdictions, since the sales tax for this transaction should ideally be remitted to multiple tax jurisdictions.

The issue can be eliminated by obtaining a multiple points of use certificate (MPU) from the state government. A sample form follows. This document accomplishes the following two items:

- The seller of the software is not required to collect a sales tax on the sale transaction.
- The buyer of the software is required to pay a use tax on its software purchase. The buyer apportions the amount of the use tax among the applicable tax jurisdictions where the software is to be used. The apportionment method can be based on any reasonable method, as long as it is applied in a consistent and uniform manner, and the method can be justified through supporting records.

A simple apportionment method that should be easy to justify is to base the allocation on the number of software users in each tax jurisdiction. Several other issues related to the MPU are:

- *Applicability.* The MPU is currently allowed for pre-written software that is delivered by electronic means. The MPU does not apply to software that has been pre-loaded on a computer when the computer is sold.
- *Usage.* The MPU is part of the Streamlined Sales and Use Tax Agreement (which is described later), so it should become more widely used as the Agreement is gradually accepted among more state governments.
- *Wider use.* A few tax jurisdictions have adopted a more broad interpretation of the MPU, allowing it to be applied to the sale of computer projects or services, usually involving the sale of digital products.

Sales Tax Holidays

Many states have instituted sales tax holidays, where there is a sales tax exemption for a few days each year for the purchase of a few items that are considered to be beneficial from the perspectives of either emergency preparedness, energy conservation, or students. There is a cap on the amount of each purchase that will not be subject to sales tax. Examples of the types of goods that may be covered by a sales tax holiday are clothes, school supplies, computers, Energy Star products, and power generators. A complete listing of sales tax holidays is maintained on-line by the Federation of Tax Administrators. The applicable Web page is:

http://www.taxadmin.org/sales-tax-holidays

Sample Multiple Points of Use Certificate

Ohio	**Department of** **Taxation** tax.ohio.gov	STEC MPU Rev. 3/15

Multiple Points of Use Exemption Certificate

The purchaser hereby claims exception or exemption on the purchase of tangible personal property and selected services made under this certificate from:

_____
(vendor's name)

and certifies that the claim is based upon the purchaser's proposed use of the items or services, the activity of the purchase, or both, as shown hereon:

_____

Check one:

☐ Single purchase certificate: Relates to invoice/purchase order # _____

☐ Blanket certificate: If checked, this certificate continues in force until canceled by the purchaser.

☐ Multiple points of use exemption certificate: Services or computer software delivered electronically for use in business.

Please describe the services or computer software electronically delivered for use in business:

By issuing this multiple points of use exemption certificate, the above stated purchaser attests to the following:

1. The purchaser is not a holder of a direct payment permit granted under Ohio Revised Code section (R.C.) 5739.031;
2. At the time of purchase, the services or computer software that is delivered electronically for use in business will be con-currently available for such use in more than one taxing jurisdiction;
3. Upon issuance of this certificate, the purchaser is relieving the vendor of the obligation to collect, pay or remit the tax due, and the purchaser must pay the tax directly to the appropriate taxing jurisdictions; and
4. The purchaser will maintain adequate records (as required by R.C. section 5739.11) as they existed at the time of the purchase to substantiate the method used to apportion the tax due on the purchase(s).

Purchaser must state a valid reason for claiming exception or exemption.

_____
Purchaser's name

_____
Purchaser's type of business

_____
Street address

_____
City, state, ZIP code

_____
Signature   Title

_____
Date signed

_____
Vendor's license number, if any

Special Situations

The treatment of delivery charges varies considerably by state. Some Departments of Revenue consider delivery charges to be service-related, and so consider them to be tax exempt. Other jurisdictions have made determinations in the reverse direction. Consequently, check with the applicable state's Department of Revenue to clarify the situation.

A company accepts exemption certificates that are issued by another state. The company has two modes of distribution. One is to sell directly to customers, and the other is to sell through retailers. In the first case, if the customer has an exemption certificate, the company is not required to collect sales tax from the customer. In the second case, where the company is selling through a retailer, if the retailer does not have an exemption certificate, the company must collect sales tax from the retailer. The latter situation is the case even when the ultimate customer (buying from the retailer) has an exemption certificate.

Streamlined Sales and Use Tax Agreement

In the preceding Multiple Points of Use Certificate section, we referred to the Streamlined Sales and Use Tax Agreement. This Agreement is intended to simplify and modernize sales and use tax administration in order to substantially reduce the burden of tax compliance. The agreement focuses on improving sales and use tax administration systems for all sellers and for all types of commerce through the following actions:

- State-level administration of sales and use tax collections
- Uniformity in the state and local tax bases
- Uniformity of major tax base definitions
- A central, electronic registration system for all member states
- Simplification of state and local tax rates
- Uniform sourcing rules for all taxable transactions
- Simplified administration exemptions
- Simplified tax returns
- Simplification of tax remittances

Thus far, the states noted in the following exhibit have passed legislation to conform to the Agreement.

States Conforming to the Streamlined Sales and Use Tax Agreement

Arkansas	Michigan	North Dakota	Utah
Georgia	Minnesota	Ohio	Vermont
Indiana	Nebraska	Oklahoma	Washington
Iowa	Nevada	Rhode Island	West Virginia
Kansas	New Jersey	South Dakota	Wisconsin
Kentucky	North Carolina	Tennessee	Wyoming

Use Tax

As stated earlier, a buyer is responsible for paying use tax if the seller of tangible goods did not charge the buyer a sales tax. A useful way to view the use tax concept is that, theoretically, *all* purchases made by a buyer should be assigned a sales tax –

which is classified as a sales tax if the seller charges the tax and remits the proceeds to the government, and as a use tax if the buyer has to pay the tax to the government. Use tax most commonly arises when a buyer orders goods from out of state (such as from an Internet store), and the seller (not having nexus in the buyer's state) does not have to charge sales tax on the transaction.

EXAMPLE

Pianoforte International buys supplies from an office supply store in Nebraska, which delivers them by common carrier to Pianoforte's office in Colorado. Since the supplier has no nexus in Colorado, it does not charge sales tax on these purchases. However, since Pianoforte would have paid sales tax on these purchases if it had purchased them in Nebraska, it should pay use tax to the state of Colorado.

As noted in the preceding example, use tax is typically paid in the state in which the buyer takes possession of tangible property. Thus, the tax is not due to the state government from which the goods were shipped, but rather to the state government in which delivery was made.

The accounting for use tax is to accrue a use tax liability for each applicable purchase. This amount is also recognized as an expense for the business. Thus, the general format of the journal entry is:

	Debit	Credit
Expense [expense account]	xxx	
Use tax liability [liability account]		xxx

The exact expense account charged when use tax is recognized can vary. If the aggregate amount of use tax recognized per year is small, the easiest approach is to charge it to a miscellaneous expense account. For larger amounts, a unique account can be created for it.

It can be difficult to determine the amount of use tax to pay. The most labor-intensive approach is to examine every non-exempt supplier invoice to determine which ones did not include sales tax, and accrue a use tax for these invoices. This can include a review of contracts and lease agreements to determine which party to these agreements is responsible for making sales tax payments. An easier approach is to aggregate all out-of-state purchases for items subject to sales tax and calculate the use tax on this total amount. Since some out-of-state vendors may have charged sales tax, this second approach tends to over-estimate the amount of use tax. A third approach is to flag those out-of-state vendors that habitually charge sales tax, and exclude these purchases from the aggregate amount noted in the second calculation method. The third approach can be refined by conducting a detailed transaction review for vendors from which large purchases were made (especially for machinery and information technology equipment). The third approach is recommended, since it should result in a fairly accurate use tax liability without requiring a massive amount of investigatory labor.

Use tax is typically based on the purchase price of an asset. Thus, if the local sales tax is 7% and an asset was acquired for $1,000, then the buyer owes a use tax of $70. The situation is not so clear when the user has constructed an asset, such as self-constructed machinery. In this case, there are several possible ways to devise the basis upon which the use tax is calculated. They are:

- The cost of the materials used to construct the asset
- The full cost to construct the asset, which includes labor
- The fair market value of the asset, if it were to be sold on the open market

Most states allow use tax to be calculated just based on the cost of the materials used to construct the asset, which is the easiest calculation method. A further concern is that many states exempt machinery used in the production process from sales or use tax, so none of these calculation methods may be needed.

Additional Use Tax Issues

Items purchased for inventory are not subject to sales or use taxation. However, if items are removed from inventory for business or personal use, they have, in effect, been sold to the final user. If this has occurred, the company is now liable to pay use tax on the items removed from stock.

EXAMPLE

A furniture retailer buys furniture from manufacturers and pays no sales tax on these purchases, on the assumption that the furniture will then be sold to customers and sales tax will be charged to the final customers. However, the store manager elects to remove several desks and chairs from stock for use by the staff as office furniture. The retailer owes use tax on these desks and chairs as soon as they are removed from stock.

A business may return goods to a supplier, at which point the supplier issues a credit that reduces or eliminates the amount billed on the original invoice. All credits received should be used to reduce the amount of the use tax accrual, as long as the credits relate to items for which a use tax accrual had originally been made.

A curious issue with use tax payments is that the Department of Revenue does not necessarily collect this tax on behalf of counties, cities, or special districts. Instead, it may be necessary to make separate payments to each of these entities. Check with the Department of Revenue to which the company sends payments to determine the local treatment of these remittances.

Buying and Selling a Business

The rules related to sales and use taxes when a business is bought or sold will vary by state, but the general concepts are as follows:

- The seller of the business must pay all taxes due at the time of the sale and close the business' sales tax account with the Department of Revenue.
- The buyer of the business must obtain a new sales tax license and pay sales tax on the tangible personal property being acquired, excluding inventory.

Sales Tax Audits

The state government may periodically send a sales tax audit team to a business to examine its records and see if the government has been shortchanged on the amount of sales tax remittances that it should have received. If so, the audit team can charge the company for the amount of the sales tax shortfall, plus penalties and interest. This amount can be substantial, and is especially galling for management, since the presumption in a sales tax audit is that the business is presumed guilty unless it can prove otherwise.

Related Podcast Episode: Episode 230 of the Accounting Best Practices Podcast discusses how a sales tax audit works and how to mitigate its effects. The episode is available at: **accountingtools.com/podcasts** or **iTunes**

A business will find that the likelihood of a sales and use tax audit will increase as its sales grow. The reason is that audit teams are expensive, and so must generate a return for the employing government. Thus, a small organization is much less likely to be subjected to an audit, simply because even quite a large adverse finding would still represent a relatively small return for the government. Conversely, a proportionally small sales and use tax issue at a large firm might still represent a major cash inflow for the state government.

Note: No matter what a company's size is, it may still be audited as a byproduct of an audit of a different organization, usually a supplier. The auditors will note any invoices issued by the supplier on which sales tax was not charged, and then follow up with the buyer to see if use tax was paid. Thus, a concentration of untaxed purchases from a particular supplier can trigger an audit.

The audits can be conducted by any government that believes a company owes it sales taxes, so the number of these audits to which a business can be subjected is nearly unlimited.

There are some variations on how an audit can be conducted, but the basic steps are as follows:

1. The auditor sends a notice of audit to the targeted business and arranges for a range of dates during which the audit will take place.
2. The auditor defines the audit objective, which is usually to locate mistakes in a company's tax compliance. Based on this objective, the auditor decides which areas are most likely to contain errors, and focuses the audit work on those areas.
3. The auditor requests that a specific date range of customer and supplier invoices be made available by the target company.
4. The auditor selects a sample of the total population of customer invoices that is considered to be representative of the entire population, so that a conclusion regarding error rates can be drawn with a high degree of confidence for the entire population. Or, if the business is quite a small one, the auditor reviews the entire population of invoices. Possible sampling methods are:

   - *Cluster sampling*, where a contiguous block of transactions are pulled for examination. Pulling these records is less expensive than transaction sampling, since records are being pulled from fewer locations.
   - *Time period sampling*, where transactions are examined within a narrow date range. This is not the most desirable sampling method, since it assumes that the transactions occurring on a specific date are representative of the transactions occurring on other dates, which may not be the case.
   - *Transaction sampling*, where a specific invoice is examined. The selected items are dispersed through the audit period. Pulling these records can be expensive, since they may be scattered throughout the population.

5. The auditor examines the invoices to determine whether sales tax was charged on all taxable items and that the tax was properly remitted to the government.
6. For those items for which sales tax was not charged, the auditor investigates whether there is a valid sales tax exemption certificate that supports the transaction. Also, the auditor examines the products purchased by the customer to see if they qualified for the exemption.
7. The auditor verifies that all funds collected from customers were remitted to the government, and in a timely manner.
8. The auditor conducts a similar sampling test on supplier invoices to see if sales tax was charged by the supplier or if use tax was paid by the target company. When neither situation applies, the auditor looks for a valid sales tax exemption certificate for the company.
9. The auditor examines purchases made under an exemption certificate and verifies that these transactions should actually be exempt from sales tax.

10. The auditor examines all assets disposed of by sale to a third party, and determines whether sales tax should have been charged on these sales.
11. The auditor compiles a list of exceptions found and forwards them to the company's accountant for review.

Note: Be prepared to defend the exemption of inventory or fixed assets that were purchased under an exemption certificate. This involves explaining how these items are used and why they fit under the state's sales tax exemption rules.

When an audit team conducts a sales and use tax audit, some exceptions will likely be found. A common approach is for the audit team to then use *error rate extrapolation*, where they multiply the rate at which errors occurred within their sampling work to the total number of company transactions. For example, if the team finds that $100 of sales tax was not collected in a sample that comprises ½% of a company's total sales volume, it will extrapolate this finding to the rest of the company's sales – which in this case results in a total charge for uncollected sales taxes of $20,000, which is calculated as follows:

$$\$100 \text{ Error} \div .005 = \$20,000 \text{ Total extrapolated amount}$$

Further, the auditors will then add a penalty and interest charge to the total extrapolated amount. This extrapolated amount can turn into quite a large assessment. The size of this potential assessment can be a significant inducement for a firm to create a detailed set of procedures for dealing with sales and use taxes, thereby driving down its error rate.

Note: Sales and use tax audits are especially likely in states that do not have an income tax, since sales and use taxes comprise quite a large part of their total income.

Errors in Compliance

An audit team may judge a number of events to be errors in compliance. The accountant should understand the nature of each of these error types in order to keep them from occurring. Here are several examples of compliance errors:

- Applying the wrong sales tax rate to a transaction
- Exempting a transaction from sales tax without a certificate of exemption
- Failing to determine whether the organization has nexus in another state
- Incorrectly reporting the total amount of sales and use taxes due for a reporting period
- Incorrectly reporting the total amount of sales generated in a reporting period
- Not paying a use tax on a business purchase that was untaxed by the seller

Audit Best Practices

There are a number of techniques that an accountant can use to reduce the impact of a sales tax audit on the organization. They are noted within the following headings for planning, behavior, and prevention:

Planning Topics

The work associated with a sales tax audit begins well before the government's audit team walks in the door. The accountant should have spent time in advance negotiating certain aspects of the audit, while also reviewing the documents that the auditors plan to examine. More specifically:

- *Schedule appropriately*. Within reasonable limits, an auditor is usually willing to schedule an audit around the schedule of a company's accounting department. This means shifting the audit away from the closing period and any seasonal activities that might leave little time to assist the auditor.
- *Negotiate the audit period*. It may be possible to negotiate the date range over which the auditor wants to examine records. There are several reasons for doing so, one of which is to reduce the number of invoice records that must be pulled from the archives. Another reason is to point the auditor at those periods when it is most likely that the company was in compliance with all sales tax requirements, such as slow periods or when the most reliable staff person was in charge of billings.
- *Use electronic access*. It may be possible for the auditors to conduct a review of the company's electronic records. This is advantageous for the company, since there is no need for the accounting staff to pull printed records from the archives, and the auditor may be able to conduct some of the work from an off-site location – which reduces the on-site disruption. Further, electronic access eliminates the risk of being unable to locate an invoice in the archives. This situation is most likely when a company has a large volume of transactions stored in an electronic format and especially when the auditors would otherwise need to access documents from multiple company locations.
- *Review certificates*. Conduct a detailed examination of every sales tax exemption certificate on file to ensure that it is complete and has not expired. If there are any issues, correct them before the arrival of the auditors.
- *Review business purchases*. Examine all purchase records for goods consumed by the company to ensure that either sales tax was paid at the point of purchase, or that use tax was paid afterwards.
- *Flag special sales*. The sales records may contain a few isolated cases where a sale was unusual, such as an order for a custom product or a large one-time order. Consider requesting that the related invoices be pulled from the samples being reviewed by the audit team, since they are not representative of the entire population of invoices.
- *Reconcile reports*. Verify that the gross sales figure stated on the company's federal income tax return and financial statements matches the aggregate

amount of gross sales figures stated on the state sales tax reports for the same period. Prepare a reconciliation statement if there are any differences.

- *Organize documents.* Do not hand the audit team a disorganized sheaf of invoices and other documents for their review. Doing so only prolongs their visit, since they have to spend extra time sorting through the documents. Instead, organize the documents in the order in which they were requested, or at least in an order that would make logical sense from the perspective of someone reviewing them.
- *Allocate work space.* Reserve space for the auditors in a room that is sufficiently far away from other business activities that they will not overhear conversations, which they might otherwise misconstrue. Always provide a workspace that has ample room; providing cramped quarters makes the auditors less efficient, which may prolong the duration of their audit.

Behavior Topics

Sales tax auditors are investigating a company to look for cases of tax non-payment, and so are in an investigative and essentially judgmental role. Many accountants do not enjoy having auditors on-site, since they feel that their performance is being judged. Also, the nature of their work causes auditors to interfere with the ongoing work of the accounting department. For these reasons, it is all too easy to view sales tax auditors as annoyances; this attitude can appear in many forms, such as making auditors wait for meetings or giving them incomplete documentation. Do not go down this path. Auditors are professionals and may care deeply about their work, so treat them with a high degree of respect. Within that general framework of advice, here are several behavioral best practices to consider:

- *Minimize communications.* A sales tax auditor is always searching for clues that could expand the potential liability to which the business will be exposed. Consequently, coach the accounting staff in advance to never volunteer information to an auditor. Only respond to exactly those questions asked. If there is any point of confusion regarding a request, obtain clarification so that only the information requested is supplied. A good way to minimize communications is to designate just one person as the official point of contact between the auditors and the accounting department.
- *Treat professionally.* Counterbalancing the previous point is that an auditor will react poorly to being mistreated, and will be less likely to resolve audit issues in the company's favor. An auditor might also believe that an abrupt and rude accounting staff is trying to hide something, and so will dig deeper into the organization's records. Consequently, treat the person(s) in a professional manner and with the utmost courtesy, but do not engage in an excessive amount of communication that will reveal actionable information about the company.
- *Review prior to submission.* Have a senior accountant review all requested items before they are given to the auditors. By doing so, any inaccurate items can be corrected and irrelevant items removed.

- *Challenge findings.* An auditor's findings may not necessarily be correct. It is possible that the auditor made a mistake in interpreting the nature of a transaction or in calculating the amount of sales tax charged. Consequently, spend a sufficient amount of time reviewing every finding made, and challenge the auditor when there appears to be a valid concern. When the auditor agrees that an exception is not valid, verify that the exception has been removed from the auditor's tax assessment calculation.

Prevention Topics

Certain best practices should be engaged in on an ongoing basis, and irrespective of the presence of sales tax auditors. The following practices are intended to improve the level of an organization's compliance with sales and use tax regulations:

- *Conduct internal audits.* Conduct the company's own sales and use tax audit at regular intervals, using the same analysis techniques that a government audit team would use. Whenever an error is found, examine the underlying policies and procedures to determine how it occurred, and fix the system to ensure that it does not happen again.
- *Examine exemption certificates.* Trace a selection of un-taxed sales to exemption certificates. Note all exceptions, where an exemption certificate cannot be found or the certificate is out-of-date. Examine the exceptions to see if the system for handling sales tax exemptions should be altered.
- *Identify contractors.* In most states, the rule is that a contractor charging a lump sum for a construction contract is responsible for paying sales tax, rather than the client of the contractor. When this is the case, clearly identify the contractor as such in the accounting records, so that the auditors will not count these invoices as an exception. It can be helpful to prepare a list of all lump-sum contractors in advance and give it to the auditors when they arrive.
- *Maintain excellent records.* One way to keep an audit team from finding any compliance errors is to maintain well-organized records that detail the sales and use taxes paid, along with the invoices on which they were paid.
- *Verify taxable items.* Routinely review the Department of Revenue's listing of transactions subject to sales tax and verify that the company is paying use tax on these items when sales tax is not billed by suppliers. Pay particular attention to taxable business purchases, such as furniture and office supplies.

Note: If there is any aspect of a sales tax audit that is vague or excessively complex, consider hiring a sales tax consultant who can represent the company with the auditors to the company's best advantage. This approach is probably only cost-effective when there is a significant risk of a large assessment.

Once an audit has been completed, ask the auditors if they found any issues that the business can correct by altering its policies and procedures. The auditors see many accounting systems as part of their work, and so can be considered experts on what constitutes inadequate systems.

Depending on the circumstances, it may be worthwhile to write a letter to the Department of Revenue, requesting a waiver of the assessment calculated by the auditors. It is unlikely that the sales tax and interest portion of the assessment will be waived, since the main point of the audit was to generate revenue for the government. Nonetheless, the accountant could point out that the business has subsequently implemented systems and employee training that will avoid exceptions in the future, thereby building an image of a contrite organization. It is possible that the penalty portion of the assessment could be waived if the letter is sufficiently persuasive.

A final note regarding sales tax audits is that a large assessment will likely trigger an ongoing series of periodic audits. Once the Department of Revenue has found a large new source of revenue, it can be expected to keep returning in later years in hopes of finding yet more revenue. Further, later audit teams will use the work papers written by the initial audit team to pinpoint the best places to locate sales tax issues, and will zero in on these areas again. Conversely, if there is only a small assessment or (better yet) no assessment at all, the manager in charge of the audit will conclude that the company is not a good source of additional revenue, and so may avoid scheduling additional audits for a long time.

Reverse Audits

A business may wish to contract for a *reverse audit*, where an outside firm is engaged to examine the organization's books to see if it has overpaid any sales taxes. If so, the company can apply for a refund and alter its systems to ensure that the overpayment does not recur. A business is more likely to need a reverse audit when its policies and procedures are poor, and there is a high rate of employee turnover in the accounting department.

To conduct a quality reverse audit, the outside firm needs to acquire a clear understanding of what the business does, how it operates, and where it operates. A prime area for investigation is whether the organization is paying sales tax on items for which it should have an exemption, such as production equipment or goods for which there is a special state exemption. The outside firm may conclude that there are areas of a sufficiently uncertain nature that the company should ask the state for a private letter ruling, which (depending on the outcome) can then be used to obtain sales tax refunds.

Additional Sales and Use Tax Topics

This section contains a few additional points pertaining to policies, training, and the use of software that can improve an organization's handling of sales and use taxes.

Policies

The following policies can be useful in the construction of a system for handling sales and use taxes:

- The amount of the sales tax charged must be stated on a separate line item of an invoice. This is a typical requirement of state governments, so that their audit teams can more easily determine whether sales tax was charged, and whether it was in the correct amount.
- A periodic comparison shall be conducted of the sales tax rates stored in the accounting system to the rates currently posted by the applicable government authorities. The intent is to ensure that the company is charging the correct sales tax percentages on its billings to customers. This comparison should be on at least an annual basis, if not quarterly.
- The accounting department must be informed when inventory is sold or given to employees, so that the applicable sales or use tax can be calculated and forwarded to the state.
- When non-taxable items are included on a customer invoice, they must be listed in a separate line item. Otherwise, it is impossible to keep from assigning a sales tax to them.

Training

Conduct a training class for those employees who deal with customers in regard to sales taxes and sales tax exemptions. This training is especially important for sales clerks who are dealing with customers that are requesting tax-free purchases. Employees should have a firm understanding of which products are tax-free, rather than relying on customers to tell them.

Software

When a business has nexus in many locations, it can be quite confusing to keep track of the sales tax rates that should be applied in every location. To mitigate this problem, consider acquiring a tax rate software package that is routinely updated by the vendor, and which provides the most up-to-date tax rate information for states, counties, cities, and special taxation districts.

Summary

The reader should come away from this booklet with the understanding that sales and use taxes can be surprisingly complex, requiring a deep understanding of when sales tax must be applied to a customer billing and when use tax must be paid on an untaxed supplier invoice. Further, the use of error rate extrapolation by sales tax auditors can result in large tax assessments that might strain the financial resources of a smaller firm. Consequently, the accountant should appreciate the need for a comprehensive system of policies and procedures in the handling of sales and use taxes.

The information in this booklet was intended to apply in a general sense to businesses operating anywhere. However, a state or local government may have unique sales and use tax laws that diverge from the information stated in this booklet. Consequently, it may be necessary to contact the local Department of Revenue if there are any concerns about the proper application of local sales and use tax laws.

Glossary

C

Combined rate. A situation in which states allow local government entities to add their own sales taxes to the baseline state sales tax rate.

D

Destination-based taxation. When taxes are calculated based on the point of delivery to the customer.

E

Economic nexus. When a business generates a certain amount of sales in a particular state.

Error rate extrapolation. When the error rate calculated from a sample is applied to an entire population.

H

Home-rule. An arrangement in which a local government requires that sales taxes be remitted directly to it.

N

Nexus. The physical presence of a business in a state.

O

Origin-based taxation. When taxes are calculated based on the point at which goods are sold.

P

Private letter ruling. A specific determination of the tax consequences of a proposed or completed transaction.

S

Sale tax. A tax imposed on the sale of tangible personal property and certain services.

Sales tax license. A permit to collect sales taxes on behalf of a government.

Sales taxes liability. A liability account in which is stored the amount of sales taxes collected from customers and not yet remitted to the government.

Single rate. When a state imposes a single statewide tax rate.

State-collected taxes. An arrangement where a state's Department of Revenue collects sales taxes on behalf of all tax-collection entities in the state.

U

Use tax. A tax similar to the sales tax, except that it is paid by the buyer to the governing entity with jurisdiction over the buyer's location.

Index